Q&A

A Summary of Biblical Teachings

Grand Rapids, Michigan

Q&A: *A Summary of Biblical Teachings*. Revised edition, © 2008, Faith Alive Christian Resources, 2850 Kalamazoo Ave. SE, Grand Rapids, MI 49560.

All rights reserved. With the exception of brief excerpts for review purposes, no part of this book may be reproduced in any manner whatsoever without written permission from the publisher. Printed in the United States of America.

We welcome your comments. Call us at 1-800-333-8300 or e-mail us at editors@faithaliveresources.org.

Mixed Sources
Product group from well-managed forests and other controlled sources
www.fsc.org Cert no. SW-COC-002283
© 1996 Forest Stewardship Council

FSC

10 9 8 7 6 5 4 3 2 1

Contents

Preface 5

Introduction: Our Comfort (Q&A 1-2) 7

Part I: Our Sin (Q&A 3-6) 8

Part II: God's Salvation (Q&A 7-49) 9
    The Bible (Q&A 9-12) 9
    The Covenant (Q&A 13-16) 10
    Faith (Q&A 17-20) 11
    God the Father (Q&A 21-23) 12
    God the Son (Q&A 24-32) 12
    God the Holy Spirit (Q&A 33-43) 15
    The Sacraments (Q&A 44-49) 18

Part III: Service (Q&A 50-83) 20
    The Ten Commandments (Q&A 53-65) 20
    The Kingdom (Q&A 66-72) 23
    Prayer (Q&A 73-83) 25

Preface

This brief summary of biblical teachings according to the Reformed tradition has been written to help children and adults understand and follow the way of salvation in our Lord Jesus Christ. It is designed to meet the reading and comprehension level of children in grades 5-6.

It follows the classic "sin, salvation, service" pattern of the Heidelberg Catechism, and the main contents are also taken, often word for word, from that great confession. Additional teachings are included from the Belgic Confession and from the contemporary testimony of the Christian Reformed Church, "Our World Belongs to God." (The complete text of the Heidelberg Catechism and Belgic Confession can be found online at www.crcna.org and www.rca.org; "Our World Belongs to God" is available at www.crcna.org.) These teachings—about the Bible, covenant, kingdom, church, and the like—were inserted in places where they seemed to fit logically.

We trust that you will find this a valuable tool in nurturing faith for all those who seek to become followers of Jesus.

Introduction: Our Comfort

1. What is your only comfort as a Christian?

That I,
    body and soul,
        in life and death,
belong to Jesus Christ.

2. What must you know to have this comfort?

First, how I sin every day
    against God and my neighbor;
second, how Jesus saves me from my sin;
third, how I can show my thanks
    by gladly serving God in everything I do.

Part I: Our Sin

3. How do you know you are a sinner?

Christ's summary of the law tells me
I should love God
    with all my heart, soul, and mind
and my neighbor as myself.

But I do not do this.

4. Why don't you do what God wants?

I naturally tend to sin,
    sometimes on purpose,
    sometimes without thinking.

I am like this because the first man and woman,
    Adam and Eve,
chose to disobey their Creator
    and became sinners.
They did this even though
    they were made in God's own image,
    good and obedient.

5. How sinful are you?

No part of my life is free of sin.

6. What does God think of your sin?

God hates sin and,
    as the just Judge,
must punish it.

But God is also merciful
and has provided a way of salvation.

Part II: God's Salvation

7. Who can save you?
I cannot save myself.
Only Jesus Christ can save me.

8. How does Jesus save you?
As a true human being,
    although without sin,
and also true God,
he was able to bear the guilt and punishment
    for the sin of all humanity.

9. Where do you learn about this salvation in Jesus Christ?
From the Bible.
It tells the story of God's saving acts
    through his covenant with Israel
        (Old Testament) and
    through the new covenant in Jesus Christ
        (New Testament).

10. How do you know the Bible is true?
Because the Holy Spirit
breathed into the authors,
    guiding them to write a true and completely reliable account
    of God's saving promises and acts.

The same Spirit guided the church to choose
    which books to include in the Bible.

And the same Spirit tells me,
    in my heart,
that this is the true Word of God.

11. How many books are there in the Bible?

Sixty-six books:
    thirty-nine in the Old Testament,
    twenty-seven in the New Testament.

12. What do you read in these books?

All about God's mighty, saving acts
    as told in the story of
        our creation, fall, and redemption.

13. How did God bring us salvation?

Through gracious covenant promises given
    to Adam and Eve in the garden,
    to Noah and his family,
    to Abraham and his children,
    to Moses and the people of Israel,
    and to all people of every nation—
        through his new covenant in Jesus Christ.

14. What are these covenant promises?

I will be your God,
    and your children's God,
if you keep my covenant,
serve me alone,

and trust in my saving love in Jesus Christ

15. Who is included in God's covenant?

Those whom God,
    according to his eternal plan and purpose,
chose out of fallen humankind
    to be his people
        in Jesus Christ.

16. How are people included in God's covenant?

By hearing the gospel of Jesus Christ,
by receiving the sign of baptism, and
by being made new (regeneration)
    through the Holy Spirit's working
        in their hearts and lives.

17. How does this salvation become your own?

Only by true faith
    in Jesus Christ.

18. What is true faith?

True faith is a sure knowledge
    of God's promises
and a firm trust
    that all my sins are forgiven
        for Jesus' sake.

19. What do you, as a Christian, believe?

I believe in God, the Father almighty,
    creator of heaven and earth.

I believe in Jesus Christ, his only Son, our Lord,
    who was conceived by the Holy Spirit
    and born of the virgin Mary.
    He suffered under Pontius Pilate,
    was crucified, died, and was buried;
    he descended to hell.
    The third day he rose again from the dead.
    He ascended to heaven
    and is seated at the right hand
        of God the Father almighty.
    From there he will come to judge the living
        and the dead.

I believe in the Holy Spirit,
    the holy catholic church,
    the communion of saints,
    the forgiveness of sins,
    the resurrection of the body,
    and the life everlasting. Amen.

20. Who is God?

God is one, spiritual being:
>eternal, invisible,
>almighty, infinite,
>and completely wise, just, and good.

This one God exists from eternity in three
>distinct persons:
Father, Son, and Holy Spirit.

God the Father

21. Why do you say, "I believe in God the Father almighty, creator of heaven and earth"?

Because God is
>the almighty creator of heaven and earth
>and the eternal Father of Jesus Christ.

God is also my faithful Father,
>the one I can trust
>>to provide whatever I need
>>for body and soul.

22. Does God continue to care for the world he made (providence)?

We trust that our heavenly Father
takes care of
everything in our world.

23. How should you think about the troubles of the world?

I should trust
>that God rules and shapes
>>what is happening in our world to his own purpose.

The future is safe,
>because our world belongs to God.

God the Son

24. Why do you say, "I believe in Jesus Christ, his only Son, our Lord"?

Because Jesus Christ,
>God's eternal Son,

is my only Savior from sin.
He is my Lord
>who delivers me from Satan's power
>and makes me his very own.

25. What do you mean when you say he "was conceived by the Holy Spirit and born of the virgin Mary"?

That the Holy Spirit
made the virgin Mary pregnant.
This means that her Son, Jesus, is
>both the eternal Son of God
>and a real human being.

26. What good does this do us?

Only someone
>who is truly God
>and truly human

could become the go-between (mediator)
>who makes us right with God.

27. What do you mean when you say he "suffered under Pontius Pilate"?

In his whole life and death on the cross,
>Christ suffered God's anger against sin,
>>shown in Pilate's judgment.

He suffered
>so that we might never suffer
>such severe judgment.

28. Why is it important to say he "was crucified, died, and was buried; he descended to hell"?

Because, by hanging on the cross,
Jesus took on himself the curse of sin.
He actually died
    and suffered the pains of hell.

He did all this to free us from eternal death.

29. What good does it do us that he "rose again from the dead"?

By rising from the dead,
Jesus
    conquered sin and death,
    won for us a new life,
    and guaranteed our glorious resurrection.

30. What good does it do us that he "ascended to heaven and is seated at the right hand of God"?

At God's side in heaven,
Jesus our brother
    pleads for us,
    leads his church,
    and sends his Spirit
        to pour out his gifts on us
        and defend us from all enemies.

31. How does Christ's return "to judge the living and the dead" comfort you?

I know that my Savior will come
    as the Judge.
He will condemn all his enemies
and welcome me
    and all his chosen ones
into the joy and glory of heaven.

32. What is our great hope?

We long for the time
when Jesus will return
    as triumphant king
to rule the universe.
Then we will live with him
    in the new creation.

God the Holy Spirit

33. What do you believe about "the Holy Spirit"?

The Holy Spirit is eternal God.

Given to me personally,
the Spirit
    unites me with Jesus Christ,
    comforts me,
    and stays with me forever.

34. How does the Spirit help us to be true children of God?

The Spirit
    leads us in the truth,
    breaks our stubborn habits,
    and makes us obedient to God
        (sanctification).

35. What do you believe about "the holy catholic church" and "the communion of saints"?

The Son of God,
> through his Spirit and Word,
gathers a community
> out of the entire human race.
This community is chosen
> for eternal life
> and united in true faith.
As a living member of this community,
> I must use the gifts God has given me
> > to serve him in the church and the world.

36. How does Jesus' Spirit help the church?

The Spirit equips the church to carry out its
> mission:
> to make disciples from all nations and
> to tell everyone,
> > by word and deed,
> the good news.

This good news is that God
> in Jesus Christ
forgives our sins
and gives us new life
> now and forever.

37. What do you believe about the unity of the church?

The Holy Spirit builds one church,
united in one Lord,
one faith,
one hope,
and one baptism.
This church includes believers
> of every time, place, race, and language.

38. Who is head of the church?

Jesus is head of the church.

He guides and serves his church through its officers:
   ministers of the Word,
   evangelists,
   elders, and
   deacons.

39. What do you believe about "the forgiveness of sins"?

Because of Christ's sacrifice,
God pardons me from all guilt and punishment
   for my sins
   and for my natural tendency to sin.

40. What comfort do you find in "the resurrection of the body" and "life everlasting"?

I trust that the new life
   I now experience
will continue after death.
By Christ's power my soul and body
   will be reunited
   and made perfect.

41. What good does it do you to learn all the teachings of this creed?

No good at all
unless I truly believe in Jesus.
Only by true faith in Christ
   do I become right with God
   and receive everlasting life.

42. Why do you say that you are right with God (justified) only by faith?

Because I cannot take credit
> before God
for any of the good things I do,
> not even for my own faith.

Only Christ's goodness and obedience
can make me right with God.
This becomes mine
> by God's grace
> through my faith.

43. Where does such faith come from?

The Holy Spirit creates faith in my heart
> by the gospel
and makes it sure
> by the sacraments.

The Sacraments

44. What are sacraments?

Sacraments are holy signs and seals
which the Holy Spirit uses
to assure us that we belong to him and are saved
> by Christ's sacrifice for us on the cross.

45. How many sacraments did Christ command in the New Testament?

Two: baptism and the Lord's Supper.

46. How does baptism tell you that Christ's sacrifice is for you personally?

In the water of baptism the Holy Spirit assures me
that I am joined to Jesus in his death and
> resurrection,
> all my sins are washed away,
> and I am a child of God.

47. Should children of believing parents also be baptized?

Yes. By baptism,
they also are promised
    that God will forgive their sin
    and will send them the Holy Spirit.
They are also marked
    as part of God's covenant
    and of the Christian church.

48. How does the Lord's Supper bring the blessings of Christ's sacrifice on the cross to you personally?

I see the loaf broken
and the cup poured out
and taste the bread and wine.
This reminds and assures me that
    on the cross

Christ offered his body
and poured out his blood
    for me.

49. Who may come to the Lord's table?

Those who confess their sins,
who believe Jesus died for them,
and who eagerly try
    to serve and obey him.

Part III: Service

50. How should you live as a Christian?
Freed from Satan's power,

and thankful for God's salvation,
I should live a new life,
> freely serving Christ, my Lord,
>> every day in every way.

51. How do you make this new life real?
By running away from sin
and by trying eagerly to do every kind of good
> as God wants me to.

52. What is this "good" God wants you to do?
Thoughts and actions that
> are done out of faith,
> agree with God's law,
> and praise God.

53. What does God's law tell you to do?
God says in his law:
1. You shall have no other gods before me.
2. You shall not make for yourself any idols; you shall not bow down to them or worship them.
3. You shall not misuse the name of the Lord your God.
4. Remember the Sabbath day by keeping it holy.
5. Honor your father and your mother.
6. You shall not murder.
7. You shall not commit adultery.
8. You shall not steal.
9. You shall not give false testimony against your neighbor.
10. You shall not covet anything that belongs to your neighbor.

54. How are these commandments divided?

Into two tables,
> with four commandments in the first,
> and six in the second.

The first table teaches us
> what our relation to God should be.

The second table teaches us
> how we should treat our neighbors.

55. What is God's will for you in the first commandment?

I should trust, love, fear, and honor
> the one true God
>> with all my heart.

I should not trust or worship
> any person, creature, or thing
>> in place of God.

56. What is God's will for you in the second commandment?

I should worship God only
> as the Bible tells me to.

57. What is God's will for you in the third commandment?

I should never misuse or dishonor God's name;
> rather, I should always use it reverently,
> praising God in everything I say and do.

58. What is God's will for you in the fourth commandment?

I should regularly gather with the church to
> worship God,

hear his Word, and celebrate the sacraments.
God also calls me to rest from my daily work
and freely enjoy the gifts of his creation.

59. What is God's will for you in the fifth commandment?

I should honor, love, and be loyal
    to my father and mother
    and to all others
        whom God gives authority over me.

60. What is God's will for you in the sixth commandment?

I should do nothing
    to insult, hurt, or kill my neighbors.
Instead I should love them
    as I love myself.

61. What is God's will for you in the seventh commandment?

I should keep the promises of marriage,
and avoid all sexual sin
in my thoughts, words, or actions.

62. What is God's will for you in the eighth commandment?

I should not cheat or steal
    from my neighbors
but do whatever I can
    for their good.
I should not be greedy
but should take good care
    of all God's gifts and freely share them.

63. What is God's will for you in the ninth commandment?

I should not hurt my neighbor
    by gossip and lying.
Instead I should love the truth
    and speak it openly.

64. What is God's will for you in the tenth commandment?

With all my heart,
> I should hate sin.

I should also avoid any thought or desire
> that goes against any of God's
>> commandments.

65. Can you obey these commandments perfectly?

Not in this life.
But they help me know
> how sinful I am,
> how much I need Christ's forgiveness,
> and how I can live a life that pleases God
>> (sanctification).

66. What do you believe about God's kingdom?

I believe God rules
> over everyone in this world:
>> both those who bow before the Lord
>> and those who refuse to bow.

I believe that God's kingdom
> was promised in the Old Testament,
> came with Jesus Christ,
> and will come perfectly
>> when Jesus returns.

67. What are the keys of the kingdom?

The preaching of the gospel
and Christian discipline.

These keys
> open the kingdom of heaven to believers
> and close it to unbelievers.

68. What is your responsibility as a member of God's kingdom?

To follow Jesus, my Lord,
    doing his will
    and trying to please him
        in every part of my life.

To tell the good news
    of salvation in Christ
    to all people everywhere.

69. How should you think of people different from you?

I should love and respect all people.

No matter what our age, race, color, or sex,
we are all the human family together,
    for the Creator made us all.

70. How should you value human life?

Since all life is God's gift,
I should care about the well-being of others,
    especially the unborn and helpless.

71. How should you think about daily work?

In all work,
    even in dull tasks,
I should do my very best
    so that I may honor my Lord.

72. What is your responsibility toward God's world?

God expects me
    to respect all creatures,
    to use nature, not to abuse it,
    and to preserve the earth
        in good condition
            for future generations.

Prayer

73. **Why do you need to pray?**

Because prayer is the most important way
I can thank God
and because God gives good gifts and the
    Holy Spirit
only to those who daily ask for them.

74. **How should you, as a Christian, pray?**

I should pray from the heart,
believing that the one true God will surely
    listen to my prayer.

75. **How did Jesus teach us to pray?**

Our Father in heaven,
hallowed be your name,
your kingdom come,
your will be done
    on earth as it is in heaven.
Give us today our daily bread.
Forgive us our sins
    as we also have forgiven those who sin
        against us.
And lead us not into temptation,
    but deliver us from the evil one.

For yours is the kingdom
    and the power
    and the glory forever. Amen.

76. **Why do we pray to God as "our Father in heaven"?**

Because the almighty God is our Father
    through Jesus Christ.
Our Father will give us
    what we need
        when we ask in faith.

77. What does "hallowed be your name" mean?

Help us to live
> so that all we think, say, and do
>> honors and praises you.

78. What does "your kingdom come" mean?

Rule us by your Word and Spirit
> so that we obey you more and more.

Keep your church strong
> and add to it.

Destroy every force that fights against you
> until your kingdom is complete and perfect.

79. What does "your will be done on earth as it is in heaven" mean?

Help us and all people
> to obey your will
>> as willingly and faithfully
> as the angels in heaven.

80. What does "give us today our daily bread" mean?

Help us trust you,
> the source of everything good,
for all our daily needs.

81. What does "forgive us our debts, as we also have forgiven our debtors" mean?

For the sake of Jesus Christ,
forgive us our sins
> just as we forgive our neighbors.

82. What does "lead us not into temptation, but deliver us from the evil one" mean?

Strengthen us by your Holy Spirit
> so that we may fight against
>> the devil,
>> the wicked world,
>> and our own sinfulness.

83. Why do we end the prayer by saying, "For yours is the kingdom and the power and the glory forever. Amen"?

Because we know that you,
 our all-powerful king,
will certainly hear our words
and will give us everything good.

And because your holy name
should receive all the praise, forever.